Stay or Move?

How to Talk to a Senior About Their Changing Needs and Retirement Residences

Marie-Claude Giguère

Published by Helping Seniors™
P.O. Box 564, St-Laurent Outlet, Montreal, QC, H4L 4V7

Library and Archives Canada Cataloguing in Publication

Giguère, Marie-Claude, 1971-
    Stay or move? : how to talk to a senior about their changing
needs and retirement residences / by Marie-Claude Giguère.

Issued also in an electronic format.
ISBN 978-0-9878473-0-0

    1. Older people–Housing. 2. Older people–Dwellings.
3. Older people–Services for. I. Title.

HD7287.9.G55 2011   363.5'946   C2011-907502-4

Copy editor: Emma Jane McKay (MudScout.com)

Design and typesetting by Isabelle Ste-Marie, Graphic designer (ismdesign.qc.ca)

This book is set in ITC Clearface

Author photo © Olivier Samson Arcand/OSA IMAGES

Cover and interior illustrations: iStockphoto.com

Printed and bound in Canada by Marquis Imprimeur, Inc.

Helping Seniors™
Experts in helping seniors relocate

"Nothing is worth more than this day."

Johann Wolfgang von Goethe

This guide is dedicated to all the beautiful seniors and their families who have trusted in me at a very delicate step in life. Thank you for nourishing me and guiding me to where I am today.

TABLE OF CONTENTS

PREFACE
My Story

I am the youngest of five. When I was growing up, kindergarten was just a half-day, and I have fond memories of napping in the same bed with my mom and having her all to myself while the others were at school. She had me at 40, so I've always known her with grey hair. I vividly remember reassuring her that when she got old (even though she was already old in my mind, I knew she would get older!), I would take good care of her.

I am now 40, so she is that much older. The desire to take care of my mom when she got older never left me, and I built my profession around helping seniors when it comes time for them to transition into a new living situation. I started my business, Helping Seniors™, when I became a mother myself, and I've been doing it for 12 years now.

Though I started Helping Seniors™ in 1999, long before living through my parents' changes in autonomy and their own need to transition into a retirement residence, their recent life changes have enabled me to understand that much better what families go through.

First, a little background on my parents: They are both very creative people (my mother worked as a seamstress and my father was a tinsmith). They are healthy (my mother is a little less healthy but she is certainly on top of her health issues), strong-willed, and have taken care of themselves very well. They are very generous (sorry – very, very generous), and they live in a small village where they own ("owned" is more appropriate at the time of this writing) an income property. Overall, they are very simple people. My dad is a workhorse who loves tinkering, driving his tractor, and making or fixing things (roofs, trailers... you name it, he did it).

Over the years, I had spoken with my parents about relocating and the different options they might be envisioning. At times, we discussed situations I was facing with clients (though I was always sure not to divulge personal and confidential information). They always seemed intrigued, and then they would comment, "You have got to be kidding! They did not do that! Why did it take so long? How come the parents are not talking to their children about it? Why are the children fighting?" Many times, my answer to them was, "It's just the way that it is. Do not judge the situation. It just is."

Little did any of us know that my parents would behave in some of the very same ways when their own time came to transition into a new living situation.

They had been talking about selling their house, where they had been living for the past 40 years. Although they had been encouraged to downsize for a while, and they did acknowledge that the time was coming, they were not ready. My mom had always said that, should anything happen to make it impossible for them to manage the upkeep of the house, they would be out of there. The time was nearing, and they knew it, but nobody could have foreseen the way it actually happened.

Things can change quickly, and they certainly did for my parents – literally overnight. During his sleep one night, my dad experienced an epileptic seizure. His first convulsions ever. Epilepsy at 78! Whomever should be thanked for the fact that he was not up a ladder when it happened, thank you!

Since that initial stay at the hospital, they've never gone back home to live.

From finding a residence, to selling the house, to moving into their new pad, my parents consulted with neighbours and friends and avoided getting their children involved.

I shared with my mom that I would love to help her and be a part of this stage of their lives. Knowing that I have assisted many people in similar situations, I was cautious not to use the "I am a professional in this field" approach and instead handled it very delicately. I drove for two hours to sit down and talk with them to see how I could help. But my mother barely took part in the discussion during that visit.

I was livid. I tried not to let it show, but it was very hard. I was frustrated. Hurt. She knew I was coming; she had seemed to be looking forward to it... why would she be doing this?

When I was growing up, I always wondered why certain information wasn't shared between family members. My mother had a habit of being rather secretive, and I never understood why. This secret-keeping was a challenge for my siblings and me during our recent issues with my parents. I had recognized it a couple of times and intended to call her on it but never did.

My siblings and I sat down for a family meeting to discuss the situation at hand without my parents' knowing (my parents had been asked many times if they wanted to sit down with us, and they were never willing). At this meeting there were no spouses and no children. Just brothers and sisters. Very rarely have just the five of us sat down together. It was a fascinating experience. We went around the table sharing our thoughts and feelings about the situation. We shared all the recent stories that we had been told not to tell or share. It was during this meeting that we discovered that my mother had been telling my sister that they planned to sell the house, "but don't tell your brothers and sisters. We are signing a lease next week, but don't tell anyone." This meeting gave us all a more complete picture of what we were dealing with. We all left on the same page.

My parents chose to keep us, their children, in the dark so that they could make their own decisions the way they wanted to make them. They called upon neighbours to help them move and settle in. It was all done slowly, bit by bit.

Although the transition only began five months before writing this, I have learned a lot through this experience. Though I would love to share this step with my parents, I haven't shared these kinds of big steps with them in the past. They bought their cars and sold them without their kids' input, they decided how many children they would have, they bought and sold their own houses and tools and gave gifts to their grandchildren as they pleased. Similarly, my parents are not involved in the discussions that I have with my husband regarding different life choices, nor do we (my husband and I) consult our two children when we need to make certain large decisions.

It's like how teenagers don't tell their parents everything that is going on, or who they are hanging out with, or what they did (I never did that as a teenager, by the way!), in order to protect themselves as well as their parents. And parents do not share certain things with their kids, also in order to protect them. The reality is that it happens all the way through life and at all stages.

I did not think I was "pushing" help onto my mother by going home to help my parents develop a plan of attack, but I think that is how she felt about my visit, and she did not know how to handle it. Silence was her method of coping.

My mom (I mention her a lot as she is more the communicator in the couple, and my dad more the follower) was happy to know that my siblings and I had met. I believe she was happy because we were able to fill one another in on the situation without her having to choose the words to do it, or deal with whatever emotions it might have brought out, from her end of things or from her kids. It's all about being safe.

This step in life with my parents has forced me to revisit the relationship I have with them. With Dad, the relationship I have is exactly the one I've always known I had – he's the man with all the answers and a good ear to listen. With Mom, I thought I had a closer relationship, more on a friendship level. It has been a hard reality check, but looking back over the years, a friendship is something I may have longed and hoped for, but that was never really the kind of relationship I had with her. In her advancing age, she is still the same person she always was. Attempts to discuss her feelings inevitably get deflected to talk of how sick the neighbour is, how the house up the street burned down or how another couple is divorcing. She's just not one to share her feelings about herself, her marriage, or her life.

An apple will become a ripe apple and not a ripe pear.

This experience, so close to home, has helped me to see and understand better, though it is not at all what I had expected to see, especially since I am in this field of work. Thanks, Mom and Dad, for the good lessons learned! And I mean that.

Now, more than ever, I see the value in getting input from professionals who are not family. It helps to have objective help, since we inevitably want to protect family and do not always express ourselves in the same ways we do with neutral strangers.

My heart and soul have been poured into this guide in order to help you find the assistance you want to provide for your elderly loved one. Rest assured that you are not the only one going through this. Although we each go through it differently, you are not alone.

Marie-Claude

INTRODUCTION

Helping a loved one (friend or family) navigate the sometimes-rocky roads of aging can be a difficult challenge for everyone involved. Determining that it is time to change a living situation, whether that means bringing in help or finding a facility, can be a painful, scary process – especially for the person at the centre of the change. Through years of experience helping people make this transition successfully, I've become familiar with some of the common signs that indicate that the time has come for an individual to make a change in their living situation. I've also been able to narrow in on the most effective ways to initiate and carry out the tough but necessary conversations around this transition.

All of this insight has been compiled in the following guide, the goals of which are:

- To give you (the caregiver, friend, or family member) clarity about the situation; determining whether or not your loved one actually needs help is the first step.

- To provide you with a step-by-step guide to help you assess the situation and assist your loved one in making the best decisions.

- To help you understand what to expect from a retirement residence.

- To help you initiate a conversation with your loved one.

- To help you understand how your elderly loved one might be feeling and what they might be thinking – this guide emphasizes a compassionate approach in order to help your loved one as effectively as possible.

Throughout this guide, you will occasionally see offset blocks of text that begin with an italicized comment and feature an illustration of a senior's face. These serve to highlight different excuses or comments that I have heard from clients over the years. At times these comments are true, but other times I've realized they were excuses given to mask fears or other emotions that at times can be overwhelming. My intention is to help you read between the lines and provide a "translation" of what might actually be being said.

I've also included a number of anecdotes, offset in grey boxes, based on situations that I have personally lived or shared with clients in the past.[1] If you recognize elements of your own situation in some of these anecdotes, it is because they reflect what I have found to be some universal themes and reactions to changes in autonomy. This guide is based on what I've learned in my years of hands-on experience in assisting individuals and their families through this transition.

What makes you think your loved one might be in need of help?

Do you find yourself worrying about the safety or well-being of an elderly individual? Are you concerned about how best to address these concerns? Or have you tried

[1] Names and other identifying details have been changed in order to protect the identities of the individuals involved.

many times to discuss the present situation and the growing need for help only to end up in an argument, arms crossed and no one listening to each other?

We never see ourselves as old.

The aging process can be slow, and we don't always feel our actual age. Sometimes the mind is sharp, but the body just isn't what it used to be. With Helping Seniors™, my expertise lies in assisting seniors with relocation, but I fully understand that home is where everyone wishes to be. A move may not be necessary in every case, but some things may need to be adapted and/or implemented within the home in order for the individual in question to be and feel safe.

> ***"Oh, I am a little foggy-headed; you just woke me up."***

I may or may not have been sleeping, but you caught me off guard, which made me a little confused. That scares me, especially if I feel like I have some memory loss, and it embarrasses me.

It is always a question of safety and security

If the person you are helping is deemed inept, then you must make the proper decisions for them in order to ensure their safety and well-being.[2] In this situation you are the "parent," the decision-maker, and you must provide and/or establish systems to protect the best interests of everyone involved – including yourself.

Should the person you are assisting be mentally sharp, he or she is still able to decide what they want, and you cannot force your own wishes onto a person in this situation. You can accompany them, point out certain situations and options, and discuss these with them, but in the end, what they choose to do is their choice and not yours, though you may not agree with it. It is important that people maintain their independence for as long as they can.

When assisting a couple, the approach is different than when helping a single person. The couple creates a team, and they each have someone to lean on and communicate with. Their care levels might differ substantially, though, and that is often a challenge. As a "team" they will try to continue to operate as they always have.

---

[2] Ensure that you have the proper legal documents required for the task at hand; discuss this with the appropriate legal professionals.

While it might not look from the outside like they are doing what is best for themselves, they are most probably operating as they always have – relying on each other is what they have always known and it is imperative to be supersensitive to this when dealing with couples. They often cover for each other and help to conceal the other's weaknesses. Single people do not always have a "rock" to lean on, so they often communicate with and rely on family differently and also have different needs.

A loss of autonomy is not easy to accept.

> "How did this happen?"
>
> "When did it happen?"
>
> "Why to me?"
>
> "All the things I used to be able to do are getting harder to do. I don't understand."

Carmella said, "I know my family does not want me to fall, so when I visit, they have me walk through the garage to avoid stairs. They also think it is faster that way." Carmella felt shut out from the life happening at her son's place. She saw the garage. "I feel degraded and that I am not worth seeing the inside of their house. I do not get to experience 'life' in their house because they want to protect me." It can be tough to find the balance between protection of a senior's safety and overprotection. The danger in overprotection is that you may unknowingly be speeding up certain processes. If an individual is still capable, they will do best if they are given space to keep doing what they are able to do. Grant them the extra time they need to accomplish tasks.

At times, physical pain is associated with a loss of autonomy, creating physical limitations (difficulty climbing stairs, for example), emotional turmoil (having to face new realities, resisting accepting a present medical diagnosis), and/or withdrawal from social interaction (not hearing and/or seeing as well may lead to an individual becoming more homebound). These are all big changes that bring with them a grieving period, and depending on the person dealing with the loss, he or she might fight tooth and nail to not accept them.

Is this still the right living situation?

Thinking about moving to a retirement residence is not easy for anyone. The person you are assisting or concerned about will most likely feel a sense of loss: loss of autonomy, loss of dignity, and loss of self-esteem. He or she may begin to feel unneeded or isolated.

When we think of moving to a "residence," there are a lot of negative stereotypes. Retirement residences are often thought of as places to die or places where everyone is old and sick. Seniors might fear that "you are just going to put me away there, it is filled with old people, it's not for me, I'm only 85, I can still do plenty of things and I'm still autonomous, everyone there is sick...." The list goes on. These thoughts are hard to overcome. Keep in mind that there are many different types of residences. While the person you are helping may have to make small compromises in some way, there is certainly a retirement residence out there to meet this individual's needs; the challenge is finding it, but once that goal is achieved, many of these fears will be put to rest.

If a move does occur, there is an adjustment period, as there is for everyone who moves. In my experience, it is about six weeks. And often the comment is, **"If I had known, I would have done this a long time ago."** Should the decision be to stay at home with care providers coming into the house, there is also an adjustment period.

Key point: Don't think of it as "placing"

Now that the weight seems to be put on your shoulders, you may be feeling overwhelmed. It's normal to feel confused about what to do and how to go about it, or to feel that you have no time on your hands to handle the situation. You may feel guilty at the thought of "placing" your loved one in a retirement residence, but a relationship does not change with a change of address. You are not "placing" the person you are assisting; you are helping them find a solution that will enable them to feel safe and remain as autonomous as possible for as long as possible. That may mean they can stay at home with some assistance, or it may mean they need to relocate. What is essential is that you find a solution that works and that is healthy and safe for everyone, especially the person you are assisting.

It is often a loss of autonomy, a major change in life, or a crisis situation that makes us realize that something in the present setup has to change.

While broaching the issue of a need for change may seem overwhelming, there are concrete steps you can take to make the process smoother and more comfortable for everyone involved. Let's go through these steps.

STEP I
ASSESS THE SITUATION

It happens slowly, often unnoticed, a little thing here and there. It can be hard to pinpoint exactly when the shift takes place, but at some point, it becomes clear that things have changed, and a child has taken on the role of parenting their parents. Your loved one needs special help, and it is hard when we are forced to admit that we can't help them – that we are overwhelmed, or have too many other responsibilities.

From the perspective of your elderly loved one, it is difficult to ask for help – we rarely want to trouble anyone to help us accomplish tasks that we were once able to do ourselves. As somebody arranging appropriate care for your loved one, you might also find it hard to acknowledge that you have reached the limit of what you can do, and that you too need to seek out help.

> *"Instead of you coming to my house, I would rather meet at your house or a coffee shop."*

The state of my house is embarrassing to me, and I would rather you not see it. I fear you will judge me.

What is important to remember is that we all need extra help sometimes, and we all need professional help sometimes. As children, we often feel guilty that we don't have the ability to care for our parents, but when parents require special care, there should be no guilt in accepting that we cannot do it all and that we must get them the help they need. For example, assisting someone with standing up can require special training to protect one's back. You won't be much help to anyone if you throw your own back out. Getting your elderly loved one the right help is something to be proud of.

Are you simply at the stage of seeing what is out there, and doing your "homework" before a crisis happens? That would be the ideal option, but we don't always have the luxury of time in these situations. Is there a real safety risk at hand that needs to be dealt with before a crisis does happen? Are you, as the primary caregiver, finding yourself totally overwhelmed, sleep-deprived, and unsure of how to proceed?

You know the person you are trying to help. Listen to what your gut feeling is telling you, since they may not be willing or able to verbalize their needs.

Watch for signs that a change needs to happen

- Are you worried about leaving them alone?

- Do you have trouble finding time to assist them with their doctor's appointments?

- Are you having difficulty fitting in both your shopping and their shopping? Their laundry and your laundry?

- Do you feel uncomfortable after visits or phone calls with them?

- Are you simply butting heads with your loved one and/or other family members about how to handle things?

- Are you seeing an increasingly disorganized home?

Have you noticed any of these changes in behaviour?

- Are they calling more often, or much less frequently?

- Do they request your presence more often or require more assistance around the house?

- Are they expressing more and more fear?

- Are they afraid at night?

- Are they hesitant to take a shower/bath?

- Do they not trust certain people they really trusted in before?

- Are they bitter towards you, or do they address you with an aggressive tone every time you speak with them?

Have you noticed any of the following signs of a decrease in autonomy?

- A cluttered house.

- Unpaid bills.

- Dressing inappropriately for the weather.

- Unclean or unkempt clothing.

- Weight loss.

- Poor or changed personal hygiene.

- Cluttered, disorganized medications.

- Disorientation or confusion.

Nutrition often slips as well. It gets harder to go shopping (that milk is heavy!), going to the store takes longer, and standing at the stove can be exhausting, so a little tea and toast solves the problem… for now. Eating is a social activity, so when we eat alone it is less appetizing, and it may become less of a priority.

Once you've established the presence of a few concerning signs, what can help to bring things back to order? How can the situation be changed so that you will no longer worry about leaving them alone at home and so that you can sit down and enjoy your visits with them rather than spending that time tending to all of their care needs?

It is hard to see the Earth when you are standing on it.

Sometimes we are too close to the situation to know what it is we need. When assessing what needs to be done, consider who else is involved in this person's care. Do you have brothers or sisters? Aunts or uncles? Are there any community services that might already be involved? Is there a housekeeper or neighbour who is present frequently? It might be beneficial to speak with others involved in your loved one's life in order to get a better idea of what they are seeing and feeling. Are they seeing and feeling the same things you are? Do they see the situation the same way you do? Perhaps they see other things that you might not see. Ask them what kind of discussions, if any, they have had with your loved one regarding the changing needs that you all see. Get a feel for the type of approach that worked for them if and when they brought up these sensitive subjects, and share with them what has worked for you.

One of my clients, Eunice, was getting panic attacks, and she did not know why. We sat down together to discuss her situation. Her dishes were piling up, her laundry was not getting done, and it was hard for her to stand in the kitchen to prepare her meals. It was only through our discussion that she realized that these issues were part of the reason for the panic attacks. So her housekeeper now comes weekly instead of monthly and has added a few extra things to her to-do list, and Meals on Wheels delivers twice a week. Eunice now feels a greater sense of autonomy, has fewer panic attacks, and is eating at least one good meal a day.

Make a list of the present needs the way you see them. Go back to that list after a couple of days. Do you agree with what you wrote? Is there anything to add or remove? After speaking with other people involved in the situation, does anything need to be revised? This list of needs is not static – with time, it changes and evolves.

Stop, look, and listen to the situation as well as you can. There are solutions out there.

IS STAYING AN OPTION?

Before deciding to suggest a retirement residence, consider whether or not staying at home could be an option. Knowing where your loved one lives, the physical setup, the financial situation, the support system in place, and your loved one's personality, is it possible for them to stay home and receive extra help? You'll need to consider who might be hired, for what type of assistance, how often, and at what cost.

> About five years ago, I met Mr. and Mrs. Keneski, a couple still living in their condo. They were 100 and 100½ years old, and were spending $8000 a month for 24-hour attendants. This amount was just for their care; it did not cover the condo fees, electricity, food, or any of the other expenses that come along with running a household.
>
> The lady, 100½ years old, sat on her couch, looked at me and said, "I feel like I am 150 today!" We had quite a laugh.

While at home, in addition to assuming all the costs of personal care, you are also responsible for all expenses involved in running the household and maintaining the building. At a residence, you share the cost of the overhead with everyone else living there.

Things to consider if staying at home is an option

- Are the stairs still manageable? If not, could a ramp or chairlift be installed inside and/or outside?

- Are the bathroom(s), laundry room, and bedroom on the main floor? If not, can this be altered? At what cost? Would this affect the resale value of the house?

- Could the bathroom(s) accommodate grab bars? An elevated toilet seat? A step-in shower (if needed)? A bath seat?

- Could a new system be implemented for medications? A "Dispill" system set up by the pharmacy? Or a box with a.m./p.m. daily sections? Different gadgets also exist to remind people to take their medication. If your loved one is diabetic, is there a system that could be put in place to remind them to test their sugar levels?

- For meals, can the local grocery store deliver the grocery order? Can orders be placed online? Could you purchase and/or have prepared meals delivered, òr have someone prepare meals at home? Is the use of a microwave and/or stove still manageable?

- Could new clothes be purchased to help facilitate the task of getting dressed? (Examples include garments with fewer buttons, elastic bands, and shirts that slip over the head.)

- Could someone come in to help with housekeeping? If so, at what frequency? At what cost? To accomplish which tasks?

- Social needs are important. Could someone come in for friendly visits (not care visits)? Or is there a day center offering activities located conveniently close by? Do they provide transportation?

- If specialized care is needed, who can provide it? At what frequency and at what cost? If they sleep over, can the setup of the house accommodate that?

- Is the lighting appropriate for the person's present eyesight?

- Could different systems be put in place if there is a loss of hearing?

- Are door handles and faucets easy to turn?

- Could a security system be put into place to help communicate with someone easily in case of a fall or emergency at home?

- If a cane, walker, or wheelchair is needed, is it easy to manoeuvre in the house? (Try to limit throw rugs or loose flooring as this increases the probability of tripping.)

- Are frequently used items kept at a manageable height?

"Oh, I had diarrhea yesterday, so I do not want to go out today."

I am afraid of stepping out of the house. At home, we know how far everything is, what walls we can use as supports, and that there is no wind or sun, but once we step out of the house, our autonomy is not the same.

If it is possible to adapt the present living environment, and that makes the most sense, then staying home might be the best option.

Things to consider if the choice is to stay home

Beyond improvements to personal care or the physical setup of an elderly loved one's home, don't forget the social aspect. Will anyone sit down with the person in question, go for a walk, go shopping, and share in their passions? This individual is still very much alive and needs social interactions, whatever their state. Make sure to consider this if the decision is made to stay put.

One of my clients said this best when her mom was in the hospital: "My mom is so tired from all the hit-and-runs."

I inquired further about what she meant by this, and she described how many different people kept coming in, doing the job they needed to do, not getting to know her mom, and then just running off. "Hit-and-runs" are tiring and often intimidating, making us feel like we've lost power and control of the situation.

"I cannot hear her."

This may indicate a hearing loss, but it may also mean an individual is unable to follow a conversation. There is no need to yell because we do not hear as well when someone yells at us. Make eye contact, and project your voice to the good ear. Take as long as necessary to make sure the person has not only heard but has understood what you are saying.

If there are high care needs that require staff to come in, do not forget that there is also the task of overseeing the scheduling to ensure that all the care needs are met. You can hire people privately to create a "care team" and oversee everything yourself, or you can hire a company that will oversee the schedule, find the qualified staff, and ensure staff is at the home when promised. Indeed, the latter option may be more expensive, but it can eliminate a lot of headaches.

If staying at home is an option but staff will not be hired, establish who among family and friends will be responsible to help. Set up a schedule to establish who will do what and when it will be done. Be sure to establish backup plans in case someone is unable to fulfill their obligations. If someone can't help out with their time, could they help financially? What is the cost related to the people who are helping this elderly loved one? What impact will it have their jobs? And on their families? These are all things that need to be considered and planned around. It will ensure better results.

If you've considered the physical environment, the care level, and socialization, and staying at home does not seem to be the best option, then it is time to discuss the possibility of a move.

TIME TO MOVE? GET INFORMED ON RETIREMENT RESIDENCES

Many of us have never set foot in a retirement residence, or if we have, it was to visit an elderly aunt years ago, and our experiences may not reflect the current state of retirement residences.

Before you talk to your loved one about the possibility of relocating to a residence, let's take a closer look at what a retirement residence is today.

What is a retirement residence?

A retirement residence is a place where people with common needs create a community and receive the assistance they need. The major goal of a retirement residence is to bring the community closer.[3]

There are public facilities that are subsidized and run by the state, and there are private facilities, privately run and owned. At Helping Seniors™, we specialize in the private facilities, and so private facilities are the focus of this guide. If you wish to obtain more information on the public facilities, please contact your appropriate local community service(s).

A wide variety of residences, with different services, different room/apartment sizes, and different clienteles exist, so it is important to identify your specific needs and ensure they are met in the residence you choose. Prices vary, though most are quite competitive within neighbourhoods if they offer the same care levels.

[3] This is my definition, with no one else's influence.

Decoding hours of care

Residences work with a "magic number." This refers to the number of hours of care per day that are needed for individual care: bathing, meals, medication, dressing, and so on.

Most residences will fall into one of these four categories:

1. Residences for fully autonomous seniors. These residences offer no services, except perhaps a janitor on site and a residents' committee overseeing the leisure activities (price range: from just under $1000 to a little over $1100 per month[4]).

2. Residences that cater to both fully autonomous and semi-autonomous clients, usually offering no more than 1.5 hours of care a day. These residences usually reserve a floor or two for clients who require more assistance, so if there is a change in autonomy, a transfer can be made within the building so that more care can be provided, and if light care is required it can often be provided in the apartment where the person already resides. A transfer is needed when more nursing supervision is required (price range: just over $1000 to about $2500 per month).

3. Residences offering progressive care, from fully autonomous to about 2.5- 3 hours of daily care (price range: about $2000 to about $3800 per month).

[4] The price ranges mentioned depend on the residence, on how they "bundle" their services, and on the daily personal care that is needed, as well as on the area of town where the residence is located and the size of the personal living space. Among all the facilities I have visited, most have competitive pricing. It is important to compare pricing side by side to see what is included in or excluded from the base fee and to see how the rates compare if equivalent services were to be added. Annual increases should be expected. Prices are quoted in Canadian dollars, based on the prices in 2011 in the Montreal area.

4. Full-care facilities, offering 2.5 hours of care or more per day (price range: starting at about $3500 and up).

Additional costs may be incurred for supplementary supervision. An individual might not need frequent physical assistance, but they may require a watchful eye or someone in close proximity to ensure their safety.

For example, you may have two ladies who are wheelchair-bound, and who need the same assistance every time they get up and out of the wheelchair. If one of the ladies has memory loss and does not remember that she requires help to get up without falling, she will need much more supervision than the lady who remembers to wait for help before getting up. This "level of supervision" is greatly determined by how the residence is built, where the nurses' station is located, and by whether the residence has more of an "open door" or a "closed door" mentality (in some facilities most residents keep their doors open, and in other facilities, all the doors to the rooms/apartments are closed).

If, for example, your parents are fully autonomous and do everything by themselves but would like to downsize, then they could probably manage in an apartment where there is a 24-hour-a-day concierge should they need help. If they have the desire or the need to have meals prepared (or at least would like the option to have meals prepared from time to time), then you are looking at a residence for autonomous seniors but with some services (where they offer 1.5 hours of care per day). If still more assistance is required by either one of your parents, then you are looking for even more services and/or care (1.5 hours of care or more).

The level of care needed is always a case-by-case situation. It is also very different to see the care needs written on a piece of paper (from a medical report or hospital summary) than it is to see and know the person. In addition, the residences use different techniques to determine the level of care (hours of care). The following will provide you with a rough idea of how the care is calculated and what might be included in the care hours:

What falls into 1.5 hours of care (the basic Activities of Daily Living, or ADLs):

- Assistance with bathing
- Assistance with dressing
- Distribution of medication
- Housekeeping
- Meals

Between 1.5 to 2.5 hours of care includes all services mentioned above, plus the following:

- Assistance with incontinence
- Transfers (help from sitting to standing, or assistance with mobility)
- Prompting to accomplish tasks
- Assistance with going to the dining room and/or activities, or orientation within the building

Anything over 2.5 hours of care includes much more supervision (staff is in closer proximity at all times). This level of care encompasses all services mentioned above, plus:

- Help for reduced mobility

- Help for cognitive impairment

- Help accomplishing most ADLs (grooming, eating, walking, etc.)

Services and Amenities

Most retirement residences offer a variety of services and amenities to their clients. These services might include things like:

- Swimming pool/spa

- Activity rooms/craft rooms

- Staff member who organizes group activities

- Pool tables/golf simulators/bowling alleys

- Library

- Internet station

- Hairdresser

- Foot care

- Regular, periodic nurse and doctor visits

- Convenience store/drugstore/bistro

Options for living spaces

Living spaces vary depending on the residence. Types of living spaces include:

- A private or semi-private (shared) room and private or semi-private bathroom

- An apartment (studio, one bedroom (3½), two bedroom (4½), and sometimes three bedrooms (5½))

- A purchased condo where care can be received (prices for these condos are market value, plus condo fees and building access fees)

Remember that the common areas should also be considered as extra space to which everyone has access.

I've visited more than 300 private retirement residences in the Greater Montreal area – everything from someone willing to care for one senior in their home, to foster homes (a regular house converted into a residence), to apartment blocks for fully autonomous seniors, to full-care facilities. Each residence is different and has its own character and feel. Even residences owned and operated by the same group of owners can vary. Why? Different neighbourhoods have different populations, different cultures, and different financial means. Residences employ different staff and have different approaches to offering services. Even a building's design and decor contribute to its atmosphere and feel. When I use the word "residence," I am taking into account all aspects: the building, the staff, and the whole range of care specifically designed for a senior clientele in the private sector.

Consider *who* you are helping

Your loved one has lived his or her life a certain way and this should be taken into account when looking for a facility. Some of my past clients, a couple, informed me that their monthly budget was around $8000 (which was quite high for that time). When I visited them at home, I saw that, despite their solid financial means, they lived and dressed quite simply. During our visits to potential residences, I avoided taking them to see places that were decorated with ornate carpeting and fancy surroundings, as they would not have felt comfortable there even though they could afford it. It is all about finding the right match. Helping Seniors™ (HelpingSeniors.ca) can help you with this task.

Remember that your loved one has lived their entire life identifying with certain groups socially, culturally, and financially. All of these factors should be kept in mind when searching for the right residence. These elements are part of the entire picture and there is a residence out there that can and will meet all of their needs, though some compromise will always be necessary (for example: a no pets policy, laundry facilities down the hall, or an apartment size that's not quite what one might have wished for).

Even the layout of the building, where the room/apartment is located in the building, and where the nurses' station is will come into play in deciding whether or not a specific residence will meet your loved one's needs.

This is a quick summary of what to expect from and look for in a potential retirement residences. If you wish to obtain more information, please consult my other guide, *The 65+ Key Questions to Ask When Looking For a Residence* (available at HelpingSeniors.ca). Once you start visiting residences, you will get a better understanding of it all. If you wish to be accompanied, professionals can certainly guide you through this transition. It is a very emotional process for everyone involved; do not hesitate to ask for guidance.

What about moving in with us?

Is having your loved one move in with you an option? Some families consider this as a possibility. Others know it would never work for them. If this might work in your situation, here are some things to think about:

- Refer to all the points in Step II regarding the layout of your house and your present setup to evaluate the feasibility of this option.

- If you step away from the house (whether for work or a vacation), who will provide the assistance needed at home?

- This is a new roommate. Both sides need to discuss how the household will work – from doing tasks around the house to paying the bills (or contributing to them). How will furniture be set up? Will you have a policy on guests coming and going? It's important to establish your boundaries ahead of time.

- How will your relationship(s) with your spouse and/or kids (or pets? Teenagers? Infants?) be affected by this?

- During your absence, will your loved one have any social interactions? What will their social life be like?

- How will you take a break? What do you need to put in place to ensure that you take good care of yourself and do not burn out?

- If you expand the house, what will the return on investment be? Will your house still fall within your neighbourhood's size "standards"?

- Would you want a separate phone line or cable for your loved one?

- Are you moving your loved one away from their doctors, day center, or social life? If so, how can these be replaced? What steps need to be taken?

Moving: Steps to take if there is a house to sell or a lease to break

1. Research potential residences.

2. Determine the residence that is preferred.

3. Decide on the date of the start of the lease once an apartment/room is available (if renting an apartment, inform the present landlord that the lease will be terminated – a three-month notice is generally required as per the rental board law[5]).

4. Create a floor plan to help you figure out what furniture will fit and what will be moved (this is handy for the movers as they will know exactly where to place the furniture).

5. Book a mover (make sure that the move date works for the residence and that you know the hours that the movers can use the elevators).

6. Put the house on the market (some residences offer a program that allows a senior to move in, with proof that the house is on the market, and start paying retroactively only once the house sells).

7. Start packing, give away items that will not be taken along and/or have an estate sale.

8. Do change of addresses (government paperwork, credit cards, post office, all bills to new address, and don't forget your friends and family).

9. Transfer phone lines and/or cable/internet providers.

---

[5] This is the law in Quebec. Be sure to familiarize yourself with the laws in your province or state before you take action.

STEP IV
SIT DOWN WITH FAMILY MEMBERS TO DISCUSS THE SITUATION

Now that you have determined the particular needs of the individual you are helping, you have made an overall assessment of the situation, and you are more informed about what a retirement residence is, you will need to decide who will be involved in the discussion with the person in question and how to prepare for the talk.

At this point, you want to know how to bring up the sensitive topic of their changing needs and the possibility of either bringing "care" into the house or moving to a residence without causing a scene, insulting, hurting, or upsetting your loved one. Be empathetic. Many emotions, fears, and losses will come into play for the person facing a change. Your primary concern needs to remain their safety and well-being.

This is likely a new experience for them too, and even if they have helped someone with changing needs or have moved someone into a residence before, they were in your position, on the outside looking in.

 "I have too much to do. I am overwhelmed"

> This can sometimes indicate depression, or that an individual is unable to do what he was once able to do and doesn't understand or accept her losses, and perhaps does not know how to ask for help.

Denis contacted me and said, "I am 88, and my wife just broke her hip. It is the first time both of us are dealing with this situation. For the first time, I feel like society does not want us. Our children are putting pressure on us. Where do we turn, and what should I do?"

Call a family meeting to discuss the situation in the absence of your loved one. This is not designed as an opportunity to talk about them behind their back, but rather as an opportunity for everyone to talk freely and honestly, and to get a better shared understanding of the whole situation.

If you cannot all be physically together, have some people join you by conference call. Use caution if you opt to discuss these issues by email, as it is harder to communicate tone and emotions and you risk being misread or misunderstood.

Throughout the process, remember that everyone has a different relationship with your loved one, and therefore everyone will have different feelings towards and about this person.

When you call a family meeting, make sure to:

- Prepare an agenda.

- Designate a note-taker.

- Celebrate your loved one's beautiful side: certainly not all is bad. If you find they are being stubborn, remind yourself that this kind of behaviour is normal – this transition is hard for them too!

- Avoid disruptions (kids, phones, pets).

- Leave all egos and animosity at the door. You are all here with a common goal: to make sure that a loved one is safe.

Families often tell me, "She/he is soooooo stubborn." But aren't we all? We each have our own likes and dislikes, our own certain way of doing things (be it the right way or the wrong way), and our own personality with our own internal narrator. This process is not about bullying or intimidating anyone; it is about maintaining everyone's safety through trying times. Recognize and acknowledge the small steps, and allow everyone to grow along the way.

Decide who will talk with your loved one

- Are you the best person to bring up this subject?

- Do you usually have this type of conversation with this person, or is it more often a sibling or family friend?

- Will the conversation be held with a group of people? Different people individually? In multiple steps?

- What do you feel would be the best approach? Remember that this is not about ganging up; it's about creating a team to see who can contribute and how.

If you feel you need help discussing the issue with your loved one, you may need to hire a professional mediator who specializes in helping seniors. It can be extremely helpful to bring in external help in the form of somebody who is emotionally detached from the situation and can assess the situation more objectively. Determine what will work best based on your own intimate knowledge of your family's communication style and dynamics. As much as it hurts, family is often too close and too threatening.

If a professional is invited to assist with this process, try to have a face-to-face meeting if possible before hiring him or her. The person's energy, professionalism, approach, and the manner in which they speak to you and your elderly loved one are very important and must mesh with the task at hand.

Remember to assess your own feelings

What are your feelings towards this whole process? Are you scared? Overwhelmed? It may be hard for you to come to terms with seeing your loved one the way they are. How will *you* feel if and when they decide to move and sell the family home? Betrayed? Hurt? Feeling a sense of loss? Your feelings are a part of this process too. There is a considerable body of literature out there that can help guide you (go to HelpingSeniors.ca for recommended books and movies).

At this point, it's time to sit down and begin to address your concerns with your loved one.

STEP V
PREPARE FOR THE CONVERSATION AHEAD OF TIME

Before heading over to your loved one's house or picking up the phone, try to put yourself in their shoes. How would you like someone to talk to you if you were going through a hard time? How do you react when people who love you talk about sensitive topics that you don't enjoy talking about? How do you let these people in? Keep the kinds of responses you would have in mind and apply these to the conversation you are about to have.

Consider how your loved one will react

When is the best time of the day/week to discuss this with them? During lunch at a restaurant? After dinner, while sharing dessert? While you are doing some type of activity together? You might consider a location outside their home, if possible, so there is no "territory" issue. It is OK to cry, to be angry, and to feel hurt, but at all times there must be respect and understanding... and always lots of listening.

Arriving unannounced is sometimes the best option; that way there is no opportunity for thoughts or animosity to build up in advance. It can help provide a calmer reaction and openness to discussion.

Be sensitive to the kinds of thoughts that may be over-whelming your loved one:

- How could I possibly *move*?

- What will happen to all this stuff?

- Where will I go?

- No one will take me like this.

- Will I be able to bring my things with me?

- Will they take control of my finances there?

- I will lose all my autonomy and everything will be done for me. I don't want that.

- Can my cat or dog move with me?

- There is way too much to do. I do not even know where to start. I do not have the energy to do it.

- What about selling the house? I cannot get this place into shape to have people visit. And then I'll have to sign all the paperwork. It's too much!

Should you want to eat a whole elephant for dinner, you will only do so if you take it one bite at a time. Go slowly. Go steadily. Go step by step.

After you respond with a "yes," your loved one may call back not long after to call everything off.

"My knee is hurting me, so it might not be a good idea after all."

There could be a sore knee involved, but the fact that you answered yes to their request may ignite many thoughts, emotions, and fears. It's easier to call everything off and not face those thoughts, emotions, and fears. Patience is best in this case. Keep the appointment and go with a light attitude and warmth in your heart. He called for help, and help was offered, but he is at a loss as to how to accept it. It is not always easy to accept help, and it's even that much harder to ask for it.

Challenging processes take time

While in the process of writing this guide, I sat down to discuss it with a friend over a cup of coffee. I mentioned to her that one thing I needed to add was a section on how to actually start the conversation with one's parents about their changing needs, since it had been suggested to me that that was missing. My first thought was that since this comes so naturally to me, I take it for granted that it is easy for others. There are many other things that do not come easily to me, though, and that is why we need other people to make the world go round.

So while having our coffee, my friend revealed that she had been after her parents for the longest time to get their paperwork in order – like their wills and funeral arrangements and stuff like that. They simply were not doing it and she was at a total loss, not knowing what to do. She planned to go see them, but didn't know how to bring up the subject again.

I sat back and said, "Well, there are a lot of questions that they need to answer before they move forward. If you are asking them to finalize their funeral arrangements, do they know where they want to be buried? Or will they be cremated? What kind of ceremony do they want? These are big questions that take time to answer. They may not agree as a couple, and if one does not want to discuss it, then they may not discuss it at all."

"You know, you're right," she said. "I want them to get their paperwork in order, but in the time since I first tried to discuss it with them, there are certainly things that they have decided upon. I just wish they would move on it and make it all happen, though."

My next question to her was: "Have you thought of these things for yourself? These are huge questions that we do not want to think about. Yes, we need to discuss them, but at what age? Are you too young in your 50s? I'm not sure."

This was such an "aha!" moment for me. I've often asked myself why it seems to be so hard for seniors to make decisions to move forward on things, and why everything seems so huge (from my perspective, that is). I understand better now.

The process of writing this document has helped me. The information you find in this guide has been in me for the last six years at least. Some of it came out of my head very slowly. Then I sat on it. I didn't work on it, but it kept festering. What was making it so hard for me to move forward? I talk with seniors on a daily basis, and had even spoken with my own parents about their changing needs.

The text finally came to me, all at once, in a moment not long after my parents' quick and necessary relocation. I could identify with my clients much more as I went through the emotional roller coaster, the family discussions, and experienced all the frustration... essentially exactly what my clients have been going through. This time, though, I lived it and felt it for myself. The contents of this guide were now mature enough to come out and to be shaped.

From the initial writing of the text to what you have in your hands today is a long process. It involved a lot of questioning, both from myself and from others. I thought my text was ready when I sat down with someone I thought could guide me in the final look and feel of this guide. What she said to me was, "I think you need to find someone to pare this down some more and give it more shape." Is that what I wanted to hear? No. I left with more questions. I was looking for answers.

I kept plugging away. The title, the cover, the layout of the text, and the final content only came to be when I had found all the answers. Some smaller answers came near the end of the process but I could not move forward at all until I had answered the big questions.

And that, my friend with whom I had coffee, is why I think your parents have not made their arrangements. This "aha!" moment answered for me the question of why it takes so much time, and why it seems so painful from the outside. There are big questions that need to be answered before certain things can move forward.

Above all, be empathetic

Make every effort to be sensitive to the situation in which this individual is living and try to understand where he or she is coming from and the steps they have taken to get to the point they're currently at.

STEP VI
THE TALK

You have carefully chosen the time, location, and person/people who will bring up the subject. You understand your loved one's current challenges, and have a strong overall understanding of the situation, including:

- Their health

- The present living environment (adaptable or not)

- The present support system

- The financial situation

Now is the time to sit down and discuss the issue. Remembering these key points will help keep you on task:

- This is being done for his or her well-being.

- It is of the utmost importance that you listen empathetically.

- Patience is essential. This process can take years!

- Provide reassurance and support throughout the whole process.

- Many services exist to help you. Talk about your situation with others. You are not alone. Find the support that you need. Hire help if you need to (make sure to interview them first).

Do not forget to take care of yourself, the caregiver. If it will help you to step away from this situation for a short time, then do so; you and your loved one can benefit from the oxygen theory: in an airplane, should there be a loss of oxygen, you put the mask on yourself before you assist the person beside you. If you need to step away for a short time to clear your thoughts, be sure to pass the baton off to someone else before stepping away, for everyone's benefit.

Tips for opening up the conversation

When I arrive at a potential client's house, the fact that I am coming over means that everyone knows what we will talk about and I know that no one wants to see me (though I know I do not bite, I know the topic at hand is hard to discuss). When I arrive, we usually go right to the living room or the dining-room table. I can feel the tension in the room. The initial goal is to reassure everyone and start with a friendly tone. We talk through the whole situation and discuss different solutions, from staying at home to selling the house (if there is one to sell) and relocating. That is why I am there.

You, on the other hand, want to either bring up this big subject for the first time, or continue a conversation that you've already started. You want to broach the subject and figure out what your loved one thinks and how they feel about the situation. Perhaps you want to suggest bringing a professional in for assistance. Whatever your goals may be, here are my recommendations for how to break the ice on the subject at hand:

Don't:

- Start the conversation with the main point you want to discuss. Warm up to it, slowly and gently.

- Raise this subject during a time of stress.

- Bring the kids along; you will have a better heart-to-heart.

- Keep pushing if what you're saying isn't getting through. If at some point tempers flare, change the subject, and come back to it later if you can, or bring it up at another time. Patience is key, and you need to make sure that everyone is safe or your discussions will not be productive.

- Watch your watch.

- Take calls on your cell phone, or text.

Do:

- Set your goal: Know what you would like to speak about before you get to the front door, and stay as long as it takes to bring up the subject and have a good conversation about it. Your talk may not be conclusive, as things do take time, but make sure you put it all on the table.

- Have the talk in person rather than over the phone if possible. If you can't do it in person, do keep all of these points in mind, as it will still help if you can apply them.

- Arrive calm and collected.

- Show up in good spirits, as your energy will set the tone.

- Make sure that you are not rushed and that you have plenty of time to get to what you want to discuss, as I guarantee that you will talk about many other things (big and small) too.

- Pick the right time of day and or week to go, and work around the schedule of the person you are going to visit (naps, doctors appointments, meal time, etc.). Later in the day might work for you but it may not be the best time for your elderly loved one as fatigue tends to set in as the day progresses.

- Set up the place for the conversation: go out for lunch, do an activity together, pop in unannounced, or stop by for tea. If you must do it by phone, try calling at a different time of day than you usually do.

- Keep the focus on moving forward with today's needs, not what could have been done yesterday, nor the losses that have occurred over the years. Stay in the present.

- Remember that you have done your homework: you've read this guide, and you may have looked into other resources that your loved one hasn't accessed. You may have a number of questions that you want to fire off – make sure to do it at a rate that can be managed by the person who is being questioned.

- Go step by step (for instance, focus on the bathing, then the meals, then the stairs – not "you have to move, sell the house and move into a residence" – that is too much all at once and would be tough for anyone to digest).

- Be positive.

- Celebrate the person you are helping: their passions, their life, and all that they carry with them.

Ways to ease into the conversation

Start by asking your loved one what they did today. One of my clients told me that it took her a whole hour to tie her necklace; she was exhausted afterwards but she was happy she finally got it and still could. Something that might seem silly to you can mean a lot to the person beside you. Tell them what you did (something funny is always good and fun to listen to).

Get to the subject or particular point you want to discuss indirectly, as in most cases it will be taken as less of a personal attack on your loved one this way.

When you feel you have warmed up enough, say, "Hey Mom, I was at work today and a colleague told me his dad just bought a bath seat (or is selling his house, or moving to a residence... fill in the blanks as needed to address your concerns) because he was not feeling safe anymore. Have you ever thought of that? How about you show me how you get in and out of the bathtub. Are you feeling safe? If not, perhaps a small change or a new piece of equipment would help you... What about looking into different options to make things easier for you, there is a lot out there and it is not always that expensive. What do you think? I am saying this because I care, and I want to make sure you feel safe at home."

Key point: Listen closely

At this moment, silence is the most important thing. Let them say all they have to say, listen attentively to their words, their body language and gauge your response accordingly. Can you push for a little more or have you accomplished all you can today? Listen to your gut feeling. Try not to push things over the edge – there is no need to go that far.

Other ways to raise the topic

"Dad, I saw the coolest thing – a walker with a seat and wheels. Ever seen those? Have you ever discussed that with your doctor, perhaps using a cane or a walker? What does she/he think?"

"Mike is going through a rough time with his parents. He says the bills are piling up, his mother needs help, and his father can't cope anymore. How are you guys doing? Should we be looking at different options for you guys? Do you need help around the house? What do you think might happen if something happens to either one of you? Do you guys discuss that?"

"The weirdest thing – I was driving home today and I swear I have never seen that building before, you know at the corner of Church and Stanley? Well, I noticed that it is a retirement residence. I am curious to know what those places look like inside. Would you want to come with me, just to snoop? Just for fun? I've never seen any of those places. Have you?"

Be sensitive to your loved one's anxieties about moving

Moving only gets more daunting as we age. Ask yourself right now: where are your kitchen scissors? You probably know without any hesitation. Your loved one probably knows where theirs are, too. Once they move, no one knows where they are, especially if someone else packs and unpacks for them.

> ### *"I simply can't move. I do not know how."*

I assisted a client, Marco, who had never moved from his parents' home. When his mom and dad died, this individual aged in place for a bit until the situation at home simply did not work anymore. The daily routine that he followed was exactly what his parents had established; nothing changed in their absence. It was only after Marco moved that I realized that he had a complete lack of knowledge as to how to start anew – from finding a new place and getting set up in a new space to learning new ways of bathing and showering, Marco was at a total loss, as everything he had ever done had been set up by his parents in the past. This was all new, from the routine to the physical setup and the decision-making. It was a huge challenge, but in taking things step by step, by respecting his comfort level and emotional space and by listening to his needs, it was possible to find and establish the help he needed.

The confusion a move inevitably brings can be tough for an elderly person. They may feel like they are losing their memory and/or autonomy, which is both frustrating and scary. Generally, there is a settling-in period of about six weeks as the individual adjusts to the new routine, the new walls, and the way the residence "works."

Many things change with a move.

Years ago, I assisted a couple, Mr. and Mrs. Brown, who were in their nineties and had been married for many, many years. I helped them find a nice place that would meet their needs. The couple had been sleeping on the same side of the bed for all their years of marriage. After the room was set up, guess what? The first night in their new place, Mr. Brown laid down on the opposite side, to the surprise of his family. He was on the side near the door, just like at home, though he ended up of the other side of the bed!

Follow your intuition

Stepping into a clinic isn't generally so bad, but often when we step into a hospital, we walk into what seems like a time warp. With its different lighting, colours, smells, and so many people coming and going in different capacities (security, patients, family, doctors, social workers, technicians...), it can be quite overwhelming – especially when we do not feel well.

In addition to all the action around us, we're walking into a new system, complete with new lingo, and those of us not wearing uniforms can be intimidated, forget what to ask, or do not know what to ask for, or even how to ask in the first place. Do not underestimate the importance of your gut feeling and your intuition. If you are at the hospital assisting your mother who is not well, remember that you (most likely) know this lady better than anyone there, and you have access to the whole picture. Your mother's personality, her likes and dislikes, the type of memory she has (we all have something that we remember better than others – some pick up on numbers, others pick up on names and/or faces). Charts will be filled out, tests will be done, and, hopefully, symptoms will be alleviated.

We usually have faith in professionals (as we should) and that is why we consult them. At times, upon hearing their advice and their comments, our heart tells us "no" and our gut tells us "no." However, we ignore our intuition because, "well, the doctor says 'yes.'" That's the point at which we begin to lose the strength of our gut and we start to lose our power, too.

As an example, when my daughter was young, she was petite. She ate well, slept well, and eliminated well. I took her to the pediatrician and he said that according to the charts (which I never follow), weight-wise, she was not on track with other infants.

"She must have a bladder infection, you must go for tests."

"But Doctor, she is healthy. I know; I am with her 24/7."
My gut told me all was OK and that she would gain
weight when her body was ready. But my gut weakened.

"The doctor must be right, oh my, I hope all is well with
her, I must go." So I took my daughter to be tested.

Now, every time I see the doctor, he says, "I don't know
what I was worried about. Look how healthy this child
is." I doubted my intuition because of a professional who
only saw a tiny fragment of the whole situation. I had a
sense that my power was being weakened, but I brushed
the thought aside with the belief that "he must know
better."

It was recommended that Edna wear a hip brace. The
brace was a basic model covered by medical insurance.
Her family did not question the type of brace, and they
went with exactly what was recommended. Later, they
learned that if they had wished, they could have
covered some of the cost of purchasing Edna a much
more comfortable brace that would have been very
much worth the additional expense. Don't be shy to ask
as many questions as you feel the need to.

We have to be careful of this when we step into clinics
and hospitals. We know the whole picture, but the
individual specialist sees only a piece of the puzzle. Ask
as many questions as possible. If you do not understand
something, ask them to use different words, ask for
someone else to explain it to you, or ask them to slow
down. If it makes you more comfortable, you can always
hire someone to advocate for you.

About five years ago (if not more), I meet with Mrs. MacAlister, a potential client, in her home. Sweet as pie, gentle, and soft-spoken, she was an all-around nice gal. She was thinking about moving, downsizing, and selling her house. She had identified special items in the room and the family members that they would be going to. It seemed like all was in place for her to move forward and start a new chapter in an environment where she did not see her late husband all the time.

Before meeting with me, Mrs. MacAlister had talked to friends, family, and different doctors. She was at the stage of gathering information and sharing her thoughts with everyone (chosen people, I'm sure) about the next step she was considering embarking on. She had the health and energy to do it, and the forethought to do this for herself so that she was in control of the outcome.

In our first meeting, one of the things she said (and repeated in every other meeting too, for that matter) is that her doctor had said that he did not think it was a good idea. Why should she move when she was so healthy, in a beautiful home where she could enjoy the outdoors?

I asked her if the doctor had ever come to her house, or discussed her mortgage with her. Was he there when the furnace guy came or when the roof leaked? The answer was "no."

Mrs. MacAlister is still at home, now worrying more than ever about the weight of the house, and her health is beginning to fail. However, every time we speak, she says that her doctor does not think it is a good idea to move. It saddens me to see that she is not listening to her own intuition and that the strong voice in her head is that of a doctor she sees only a couple times a year.

Try to prevent a crisis

We all know we are slowly aging. We manage with what we have as best we can, but at some point, things start slipping. It is best to face reality before it hits us in the face. Too often in my years of working in this field, I've seen people let the years go by without planning or looking ahead. I've seen people stalled by other people's comments and fears, letting these external forces overpower the wisdom of their own intuition. There is nothing wrong with looking into different options even if we may not need them today. By being proactive and researching different resources or residences, we can move forward with more confidence and a solid sense of what's out there. There is nothing worse than having a family member or friend fall ill and go to the hospital and then not be able to go back home. Now what? They have little energy to pack boxes and sort through years of belongings, and you have a full-time job. The hospital is pushing them out the door. Ugh!

Be prepared.

Consider the story about a frog in hot water: If a frog is placed in boiling water, it will jump out, but if it is placed in cold water that is slowly heated, it will not perceive the danger. Humans do the same – slowly, slowly, over time, we adjust, tweak, ignore, and stay in place. It's never too early to get informed and to begin planning, and there is no need to live in fear.

While the task before you may seem overwhelming, remember to take it step by step. Give yourself time to reflect on the current living situation, asking yourself and others what might be the best option(s).

If you indeed decide to talk with your loved one about relocating, carefully plan and research before sitting down to have the conversation. Visualize yourself having the conversation with them ahead of time so you won't be at a loss for words when you're actually in the moment. Once you're supported with solid information and a well-planned approach, you will feel more confident and secure in assisting them.

My grandmother has Alzheimer's or memory loss. How do I talk to her about moving?

Obtain support from your local Alzheimer's society. It is not easy, as there tend to be lucid moments and less lucid moments. Safety is the biggest issue, so apparent risks including fire, falling, and not being able to locate home and return there safely after an outing need to be addressed as soon as possible and you need to find the proper support – perhaps even a support group.

How do we present the option of moving when someone is totally resistant to the idea?

If it's clear that staying at home isn't an option, present the option of trying out a residence before "buying it." Some facilities offer short-term stays, with rates either by day or by week. Have your elderly loved one go try it out just for a week or so, ideally in a place that could become a long-term solution, a place where they can fit in and feel comfortable. Present the stay as a little vacation, and make sure it is long enough for them to get a good feel for the residence. Another option is to enlist the help of a professional who can help facilitate the discussion.

How can I tell if a residence is good?

Go visit. Ask as many questions as possible. Observe how the staff interacts with the residents. Take note of how the residents are groomed and dressed. Sit down for a meal in the dining room. You can learn a lot about a place from your experience in the dining room; pay attention to the service you receive, the quality of the food, the interaction between staff and residents, the clientele that lives there and the types of conversations that you hear around you. Make sure to sit with the best possible view of the whole room so that you get a broad range of input. Also, don't hesitate to ask for references from family members of other residents, and see if you can speak with people who live there when you visit.

What should be considered when planning the ideal timing of a move?

There is no time of year that is better than any other. I do recommend scheduling a move-in during the week, as the staff is usually more stable then than on weekends and you may obtain more answers from them if you need assistance. Some movers also charge a little less during the week and when it is not too close to the end or beginning of the month.

Are there waiting lists?

More often than not, waiting lists are for larger apartments, one or two bedrooms (3 ½, 4 ½) or larger. Why? The people living there are usually more autonomous so they tend to stay in place longer, and there are fewer people coming and going. Waiting lists can be tricky, though, because a person could have been on the waiting list for a while and may have moved to another address, or they may be waiting for a specific floor or apartment. If they have moved and the list hasn't been updated then it is not accurate. If you are not as picky as the next person on the list, you may have access to an apartment quicker than they do.

Who should I ask to speak to if and when I call a residence, and what information do they need?

Ask to speak with the rental agent, or the person who oversees admissions (for a higher-care facility). They can usually inform you of the cost and what is currently available. They will want to know about the person on whose behalf you are calling, what the present situation is, what care/assistance is needed at this point, and whether you have a specific time frame for a move.

Can we bring my Mom's furniture?

Some places do come fully furnished, and often the places that offer more care provide at least a hospital bed, which makes it easier for the staff and also for the person receiving the care. In apartment-type facilities, appliances are sometimes included but furniture rarely is. If possible, do bring in your loved one's furniture, since it helps the environment feel more like home, complete with their smells and their comfortable things (like picture frames, or a favourite cozy chair), all of which will help with the process of settling in.

Will they control my parents' finances in a private facility?

At most, they may ask to see last year's income tax report to ensure that they can pay for the agreement they are about to get into, although in my experience this happens primarily in facilities that are for a lower-income clientele or that are run by special programs with the municipality and/or government. Other than that, it is rare for a residence to look at an individual's finances – as long as they are paid on time, there is no need for them to get involved (in this respect, it is like a regular apartment building).

What are the roles of the professionals listed below and where and when are you likely to encounter them?

Physiotherapist: A physiotherapist helps to strengthen muscle groups that are weakened or injured. They can assist following an operation and also work on injury prevention. They generally work in hospitals or clinics, but some do home visits.

Occupational Therapist: The role of an occupational therapist is to help individuals accomplish day-to-day tasks, and to encourage independence within the existing setup. They will assess a patient's needs as well as the environment. For example, an occupational therapist would be best suited to come to the home to evaluate the setup of the bathroom to recommend a specific elevated toilet seat and/or bath seat.

Most rehabilitation centers and hospitals have occupational therapists. Some occupational therapists also work in private clinics and may be open to arranging home visits.

Social Worker: A social worker will assess the living conditions/environment/situation of the person in question to ensure optimal quality of life. They can assess a person's level of aptitude, prepare paperwork for homologations and/or curators (when a person is deemed inept there are a number of steps to follow to make this official and put others in charge), and they can also do an assessment of needs (in order to identify what type of care/assistance is needed). Hospitals will often have social workers coordinate the discharge of a patient, and they can also be hired privately to perform assessments and/or prepare specific paperwork/reports.

Care Manager: The care manager is the person who oversees the whole care approach. They are in charge of coordinating staff to come in to provide hands-on care; they ensure medical appointments are booked; they set up transportation to and from appointments; they ensure that prescriptions are filled and properly in place; and they oversee the care team. Care managers can sometimes be found in retirement residences, and they can also be hired privately.

If you believe one or more of the professionals listed above could be helpful for your loved one, find the assistance you need by speaking with your doctor, community organizations, and friends and colleagues, or by doing an online search.

Can my Dad still smoke and drink in a residence?

This is a case-by-case situation. It depends on your father's level of autonomy and also on the setup and rules and regulations of the residence. To save yourself time, be up-front about specific needs such as these, as some facilities have strict regulations for different reasons. Be honest about your father's character and any needs or behaviours that are particular to him; there is no reason to hide any information at any point.

Acknowledgments

Thank you, Denise Desmeules, for the many hours you sat there listening to me talk about this guide and for holding me accountable for "homework." Peter Eusanio, you egged me on, and I've loved every minute of our heated discussions about our industry. Thank you for that.

Many thanks to the people who are good with words: Jaimie Franchie, thank you for helping me put order to the initial text. Nicole Thevenet, thank you for your great comments and helpful insights. Mark Bromby, this guide would have had a very different feel if I had not shared it with you when I did; thank you so much for your input. And thanks to Debbi Pomerantz, my sister-in-law, for keeping me in check and helping make this guide a more enjoyable read!

Surrounding yourself with great people who know what they are doing and can guide you through to the final step is price-less. Emma Jane McKay, I looked high and low, and no one knew what I was asking for.... I asked you just a few questions to see if you could help and you fired back 20 times more. I knew I had found the help I was looking for. Thank you for all your great questioning – it came to me at a point when I was ready to answer!

Thanks to Isabelle Ste-Marie, who is responsible for the look and feel of this document. You enhanced the text with a balance of poise and creativity. Thank you so much for your patience and fabulous work.

Mom and Dad, your generosity has no measure. Your continuous support is a constant presence in my life. Mom, you will never know how much it meant when you phoned me to ask for help sorting through and disposing of your sewing supplies as you prepared to move out of the house. Your sewing room was a room in the house where you and I communicated on a different level, something that I know you held (hold) very close to your heart. Thank you both for offering me such a great base.

To the two little people in my life, Olivia and Daniel, if it were not for you I am not sure this guide would exist. On a daily basis, you help me stop and smell the roses and/or caterpillars, and it always puts a huge smile on my face.

To my husband Rob, I thank you for being such a great man for me. As my total opposite, you force me to try and see things in different ways.

To all the great people who surround me with good energy, friendly smiles, and professional approaches, you nourish me and encourage me to be the best I can possibly be. It means a lot to me. Thank you.

About The Author

Marie-Claude Giguère has a BA in Recreation and Leisure from the University of Ottawa and went on to become a chartered real estate broker. After having worked both as the director of activities in a retirement residence and in group homes with adults with intellectual handicaps, she founded Helping Seniors™ in 1999. In her spare time, she volunteers as president of a board of directors for a seniors' centre and is also involved at her children's school. She resides in Montreal with her husband and two children.

"Things are not always easy, but they are as hard as we make them."

-*Marie-Claude Giguère*

Helping Seniors™ specializes in helping seniors and their families in three ways:

- **Helping Seniors** find the proper services to help them maintain their autonomy at home.

- **Helping Seniors** find the appropriate private retirement residence in the Greater Montreal area.

- **Helping Seniors** sell their home.

Helping Seniors™ provides friendly and trustworthy assistance:

- We consult with the senior and their family to evaluate the present situation.

- We research options (either at-home services or retirement residences) and visit all residences before referring them to ensure they meet our clients' needs as well as our own quality standards.

- We accompany the senior and family on visits to potential residences.

- We help sell the house and coordinate the whole move.

- We follow up with all involved after the move (senior, family, and residence).

Helping Seniors™ is there every step of the way to take care of all the legwork and lift the weight off of everyone's shoulders.

Visit us online at HelpingSeniors.ca